Song of Trusting the Heart

Song of Trusting the Heart

A CLASSIC ZEN POEM FOR DAILY MEDITATION

TAMARACK SONG

ART BY JAN ZAREMBA

First Sentient Publications edition 2011

A paperback original

Cover design and book design by Kim Johansen, Black Dog Design, www.blackdogdesign.com

Library of Congress Cataloging-in-Publication Data

Song, Tamarack, 1948-
 Song of trusting the heart : a classic Zen poem for daily meditation /
Tamarack Song ; artwork by Jan Zaremba. -- 1st.
    p. cm.
   Summary: "An adaptation of an ancient Chinese scripture beloved by sages
and considered a cornerstone of Zen Buddhism"-- Provided by publisher.
 ISBN 978-1-59181-175-6 (pbk.)
 1. Sengcan, d. 606. Xin xin ming. 2. Spiritual life--Zen Buddhism. I.
Zaremba, Jan, 1941- II. Sengcan, d. 606. Xin xin ming. English. 2011. III.
Title.
 BQ9288.S463S66 2011
 294.3'4435--dc23
                        2011030897

Printed in the United States of America

10 9 8 7 6 5 4 3 2 1

SENTIENT PUBLICATIONS, LLC

A Limited Liability Company
1113 Spruce Street
Boulder, CO 80302
www.sentientpublications.com

Dedicated

to those who struggle to know trust

and to find the place of heart.

Contents

9 . . . . . List of Illustrations

11 . . . . . Acknowledgments

13 . . . . . Introduction: *Alone in a Sea of Humanity*

15 . . . . . Origin: *Ancient Well, Modern Thirst*

19 . . . . . How to Use This Book

23 . . . . . The Artwork: *From Soot to Life*

25 . . . . . Song of Trusting the Heart

APPENDICES

85 . . . . . I. A Word's Incredible Journey

87 . . . . . II. Layers of Meaning: *The Art of Translating Song of Trusting the Heart*

91 . . . . . Suggested Reading

93 . . . . . Notes

97 . . . . . The Author

99 . . . . . The Artist

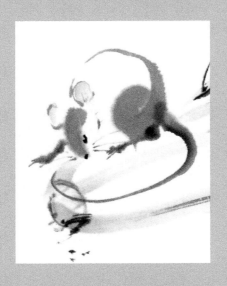

Illustrations

Page 8.   Detail from White Mouse and Green Cabbage, 2009

Page 18.   Detail from The Moon Like a Pearl, 2007

Page 22.   Detail from A Thousand Years of Happiness, 2010

---

1. Summer Day, 2009
2. Cloud Dragon, 2008
3. The Exasperation of Daily Life, 2010
4. True Independence, 2009
5. Taoist Riding the Tiger, 2007
6. That Look! 2010
7. A Word to My Admirers, 2010
8. The Emperor of the World Arrives, 2009
9. Calligraphic Birds, 2010
10. Like Flowers by the River, 2001
11. A Collector of Fine Things, 2006
12. Deer Chasing a Cloud, 2008
13. Mount Fujisan, 2009
14. The Life of the Illiterate Hermit, 2005
15. Gordian Bird Sings Knot, 2010
16. Symbol of Success, 2006

17. Rooster Challenging a Rock, 2009
18. Sumo Wrestler, 2008
19. Light in All Directions, 1988
20. Between Heaven and Earth, 2007
21. Po-Mo (Splashed Ink), 2009
22. "If You Blink You'll Miss It," 2008
23. Cézanne Meets Fan Kuan, 2005
24. Two Birds Uncertain about Heisenberg, 2008
25. Selflessness, 1998
26. The Last Chapter in the Life of an Insect, 2010
27. White Mouse and Green Cabbage, 2009
28. Like an Arrow Among Pines, 1995
29. Emptiness and Bliss, 2010

Appendix I. Detail from Migrating Birds, 1996

Appendix II. Scholar Reading Under a Tree, 2006

Page 97.   Portrait of Tamarack Song, 2010

Page 99.   Selfportrait of the Artist at Work, 2006

The Chinese terms found herein are Standard Mandarin, also known as Pǔtōnghuà (or Common Speech, 普通話) in the People's Republic of China (PRC), where it is the official language. Latin alphabet transliterations are in the pīnyīn system (拼音), which since its development in 1958 by the PRC has gradually replaced Wade-Giles (in use since the late 1800s) to become the international standard. Wade-Giles terms still in common usage appear in parentheses after the pīnyīn. Of the two standard sets of Chinese characters, simplified (簡體中文) and traditional (繁體中文), this text employs traditional.

Acknowledgments

My friend Michael Patterson is not content with just being inspired. When he came across a version of *Song of Trusting the Heart* and was touched by it, he had to share it with others. I was one of them, and for that I am deeply grateful.

Thanks to my editors, Jessica Leah Moss and Margaret Traylor, you never see the wheeze and wobble of my writing. They know my abilities better than I do, which is why it sometimes appears that I work for them rather than they for me. The research and writing was made possible by funding from The Old Way Foundation, which is sustained by contributions from those who support my work.

A book is only bland pages of black words, unless those words leap off and embrace the heart of the reader. My mate Lety Seibel, along with prototype designer Pat Bickner of A New Leaf Creative Services and general designer Kim Johansen of Black Dog Design, performed the dynamic marriage of beauty and function that gave these words their spirit. Publisher Connie Shaw envisioned this book in its final form and judiciously guided it to completion.

She inspired me to seek out the singular Jan Zaremba to illustrate the text.

My heartfelt appreciation goes to everyone involved, whether or not I was able to recognize you here, for your role in bringing the ageless wisdom of this scripture to the seekers of our day.

Alone in a Sea of Humanity

WE HUMANS MAY BE THE ONLY CREATURES TO HAVE DEVELOPED two diametrically opposed lifestyles: self-oriented and group-oriented. Prior to the advent of agriculture, people lived as hunter-gatherers in tight-knit clan groups. To this day, the few surviving hunter-gatherer peoples are still group-focused, while modern people are largely self-focused.

For 97 percent of the time humankind has existed, we have organized ourselves into small, cooperative extended families,[1] and we have lived in balance with our environment. In the very brief span of our hierarchical, industrialized existence, we have systematically destroyed a good portion of the very world that sustains us. In addition, we have created what I find to be the most sinister of human conditions: chronic loneliness. I believe this to be the root cause of much of our personal and social malaise, including crime, depression, and suicide.

One approach to our problem is to attempt fixing it, and another option is to return to what has worked for us in the past.

There is yet another way, which rather than a choice between this and that, is to reconnect with the essence of what it is to be human. This approach circumvents the morass of using philosophy, politics, and the sciences as tools to finding our way. When there is no search, no roadmap is needed; when there is nothing to fix, no tools are required.

How does one reconnect with the fundamental self? The answer, according to a few who have stepped aside from the search, does not come from posing the question. All one needs to do, they say, is *be*. In fact, it is inaccurate to say that being is something one "needs to do." Rather, it is the result of *desisting* from doing: from pursuing truth, justice, peace, and comfort. The void thus created fills with the essence of being—with the song of trusting the heart.

The lyrics of the song you already know: they are the song of your heart, embossed in its folds from the moment you came into being. The verse on the coming pages is only a reminder of this song; and when you come to trust in it, this book has served its purpose and you can pass it on to another seeker. Then only the melody will be missing, which you will sing with others when you come together in a trusting circle and let the voices of your hearts spring spontaneously forth.

Ancient Well, Modern Thirst

THE HEART IS BOTH THE ESSENCE AND MEANS OF LIFE. IN THE same way, Zen is the essence of Buddhism[2] and the means of Zen is inner guidance. We in the West have no indigenous tradition of attaining enlightenment through inner guidance. Rather, our religious traditions—Hinduism, Christianity, Islam, and Judaism— offer belief and devotion as the means to enlightenment. To fill the gap, we imported Zen from Japan. For nearly two hundred years, knowledge of Zen stayed largely in academic and intellectual circles. The liberal cultural environment of the past forty years has opened the doorway for Zen, which is currently experiencing a dramatic surge in popularity.

Commonly thought to be of East Asian origin, Zen actually has Indo-European roots (see Appendix I). Modern Zen originated as a reform movement in sixth-century China (where it was known as Chán) in response to the overbearing structure, complexity, and opulence of the organized religion that Buddhism had become. The purpose of the Zen movement was to help people return to the experiential essence of life[3]—what some Native American people call the *Beauty Way*—by cutting through all illusion and dwelling in the truth of the now. Zen embodied much of our preagricultural world view and approach to self discovery, which might otherwise have been lost.

To its core, Zen is antiauthoritarian and liberating from the confines of rational thinking.[4] Zen achieves this through what D. T. Suzuki describes as being "provokingly evasive."[5] The following ancient Zen proverb illustrates the provocative:

> Do not think, "The clouds have passed; how bright the sky has become!" For the bright sky has been there all the time.[6]

In ironic contradiction to its own founding principle of steering clear of the hallmarks of religion—formal studies, observances, and teachers[7]—the Zen movement soon coalesced into a religion in its own right. Yet thanks to the dedication of ancient scribes, we can go back to the dawn of reawakening in sixth-century China and draw inspiration from the early Zen masters. (Even though the term *Zen master* is in common usage, it would appear to be an oxymoron, as Zen practitioners are nonhierarchical. A "master" is more likely to see himself merely as one who is—or isn't.)[8] Because they were inspired by a political and cultural environment comparable to ours, their words can appropriately guide us today.

Perhaps the most profound and encompassing statement of Zen awareness is the poem titled *Xìnxīn Míng* (*Hsin Hsin Ming*, 信心銘) or *Song of Trusting the Heart*,[9] which is attributed to Jiànzhì Sēngcàn (Chien-chih Seng-ts'an, 僧璨), the third Zen (Chán) patriarch of China, who lived in the sixth century A.D. I was immediately drawn to the poem because it so clearly and eloquently expressed what I had learned about the essence of life from the native people, wolves, and other wildlings I have been privileged to live with for most of my life. In 1975 I sat on a high mountain with Hopi elder Thomas Banyacya, who described the remarkable similarities between Hopi and Tibetan Buddhist traditions. His words bore an uncanny resemblance to verses from *Xìnxīn Míng*.

I found several of the existing *Xìnxīn Míng* translations to be beautiful pieces of literature, yet there was not one that I felt completely expressed the original spirit of Zen (more in Appendix II). I studied what I considered to be the five most authentic translations—R. H. Blyth's[10] and Richard B. Clarke's[11] from the original Chinese, the version found in *The Perennial Philosophy* by Aldous Huxley,[12] and a couple of surviving partial translations whose origins have been lost to time. Looking at each as a string of pearls, I selected the most beautiful gems from each and thoughtfully strung them together with the thread of modern vernacular to create this version.

Song of Trusting the Heart WAS WRITTEN IN TWENTY-NINE STANZAS, probably to synchronize with ancient China's 29–30 day lunar calendar month.[13] The stanzas are numbered to correspond with the days of the lunar cycle. For daily meditation, read one stanza each day, beginning on the new moon. The lunar images accompanying the stanzas will help keep you in touch with the moon's rhythm, which was a major part of the culture that bore the scripture. To keep track of the lunar month's days, you can use any standard calendar that includes the lunar cycle, or you can use a lunar calendar. Number the days to correspond with the stanzas in the book, starting with the new moon.

The stanzas can be smoothly incorporated into the reflective or meditative routine you already practice. Many find it convenient and comforting to have an inspirational text at their bedside for morning or evening contemplation, and *Song of Trusting the Heart* lends itself well to this practice. You may wish to light a candle, burn incense, or play some music that encourages relaxation and openness. Or you might like to find a quiet and comfortable outdoor setting. You can carry the text in your purse, pack, or glove compartment, or keep a copy at work, so that it will be on hand whenever the moment is right.

Most religious and spiritual practices have rich reflective traditions that focus on finding inner peace, enhancing devotion, or cultivating a connection with the self or greater consciousness. At the heart of these traditions is a desire for reconnection, deeper understanding, or greater awareness. *Song of Trusting the Heart*'s universality makes it adaptable to a range of traditions, as well as to secular meditation.

Buddhist tradition has two meditative approaches: one to focus attention on a single point and the other to develop insight into the nature of reality. With Buddhist philosophy permeating *Song of Trusting the Heart*, its verses are fitting inspirations for both forms of meditation.

Yet another Buddhist (as well as Hindu and Jainist) meditative tradition centers on the practice of Yoga. Meditation is one of the means to achieving traditional Yoga's objective: uniting the individual with the universal. The *Yoga Sutras*, a set of guiding principles attributed to the second century BCE,[14] are foundational to Yogic practice and widely used as a meditation guide. *Song of Trusting the Heart* is a worthy complement to the sutras, as well as serving to clarify their message.

In many traditions, prayer is used as a form of meditation. The Christian *Lectio Divina*, or Sacred Reading, involves the slow reading of a scripture, followed by a quiet period to contemplate the scripture's deeper meaning.[15] Islam, in particular its Sufi branch, has a similar practice called *dhikr*: the recitation of the names of God or scriptural passages.[16] In Christianity and Islam, as well as Judaism, basic prayer is regarded as a way to grow closer to God. In Judaic tradition this "cleaving" is known as *dveikus*.[17] *Song of Trusting the Heart* can lend itself well to any of these practices.

Aboriginal drumming, dance, and chant are used worldwide to encourage the meditative state. *Song of Trusting the Heart* can become more awareness-raising when spoken or chanted to the rhythm of the drum. Repetitively chant one line, or dance slowly while the scripture is recited to the accompaniment of the drum.

As the scripture states, *There is nowhere that truth is not*. Try playing a recorded version of the scripture while exercising or practicing yoga. Recite the scripture while walking a labyrinth, using prayer beads, or taking in a glorious sunset. Be spontaneous and creative with your use of the text and you could well find that *all is vibrant, clear, and spontaneous*.

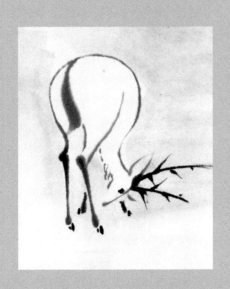

From Soot to Life

JAN ZAREMBA, MASTER OF JAPANESE BRUSH PAINTING, CREATED the illustrations for *Song of Trusting the Heart*. Jan is amused by the desire of young artists to develop their own style. "I am not trying to be heard," he says, "I am trying to listen." His joy is to communicate with every artist of the past, all the way back to the Sung Dynasty, in his own pictorial language. Jan's techniques are drawn from the classic East Asian painting traditions, particularly ink and wash. In the West it is commonly known by its Japanese name *sumi-e* (墨絵), and in China it is called *shuǐ mò huà* (水墨画).

The black ink (sumi), which is made from the soot of pine trees or tung tree oil, with the addition of deer-horn glue and fragrance, is ground afresh for every painting. The particles are so fine that they immediately penetrate the fibers of the absorbent rice paper. Varying the shade and texture of the ink, the artist evokes its expressive range. This is not black and white painting— the gamut ranges from dots like burnt lacquer to nearly invisible shining mists.

The tools of ink painting have been refined for a thousand years. The result is a medium so sensitive that it can register the slightest variation in pressure and speed, which leaves no room for corrections or revisions. In Jan's words, "Rather than applying paint to a surface, the sumi-e master performs an uninhibited dance with the brush. He captures the vitalizing force and essence of his subject by *writing* the painting. The speed of execution, the mood of the painter, even his personality are discernible from a single brush stroke."

In the Eastern view of the world, where consciousness pervades everything, humans do not dominate life. They are simply participants, and this perception of belonging results in artwork that engenders a sense of immersion. "You paint the branch well and you hear the wind,"[18] stated eighteenth-century Chinese Zen painter Jīn Nóng (Chin N'ung, 金農).

These works of art are not meant to illustrate or explain the text. Rather, they condition the mind to accept a truth which cannot be understood, but which is constantly in front of our eyes.

> Thought, anyway, would be useless
> on what thought cannot fathom.

Song of Trusting the Heart

1

The Beauty Way[19] is not difficult

for those who have no preferences.

When there is no love and hate

everything becomes clear and visible.

However, make the least distinction

and the known and the unknown will be

flung a world apart.

2

If we wish to see the truth

let us be not pro or anti anything.

To pit like against what we dislike

is the imbalance of the ego.[20]

When the truth of things is not known,

the heart is in torment, the mind will not rest.

3

The Beauty Way is perfect like all of creation

where nothing is lacking and nothing is in excess.

It is only when we choose to accept or reject

that we go blind to the true nature of things.

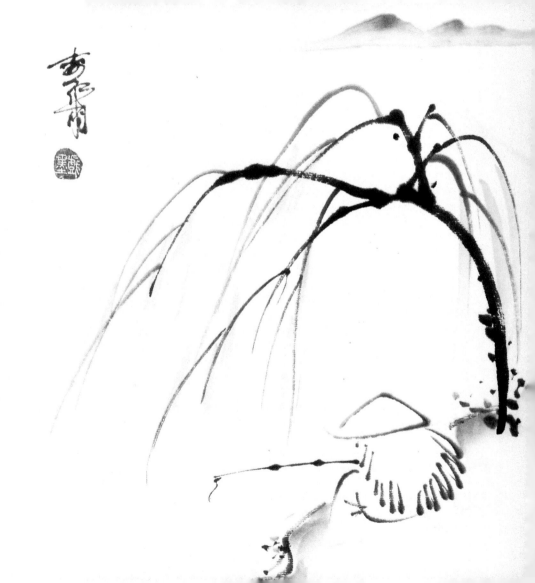

Live neither in the entanglements of outer things
nor in the inner realm of emptiness.
Be in balance[21] with the oneness of things
and such illusions will naturally disappear.

When we try to replace activity with passivity
the very effort returns us to activity.
As long as we dwell in either extreme
we will not know the Beauty Way.

6

Without knowing Balance

we will strive to deny external reality

thereby asserting it

or we will strive to assert inner emptiness

thereby denying it.

7

The more we think and talk about truth
the further we wander from the truth.
When we stop the mind's drive to know
there is nothing we cannot know.

8

To return to the heart is to find meaning,
to pursue appearance is to lose our soul.[22]
The moment we return to our heart
we transcend both appearance and emptiness.
We see that the activities of the empty world
looked real only because of our blindness.

9

Studiously avoid searching for truth;
instead merely cease to cherish beliefs and opinions.
Even a trace of this and that, right and wrong,
and the heart will be lost to confusion.

10

Be not attached even to Balance

and the mind will be at peace.

Then nothing can offend

because it ceases to exist

when we are in the Beauty Way.

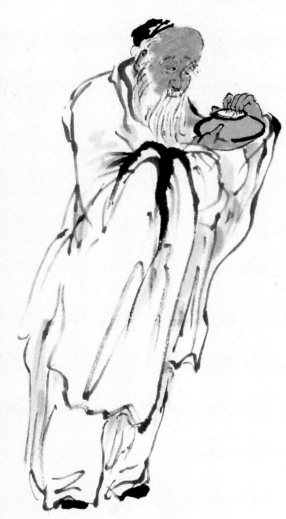

Objects become our focus because

we make them the subject (of our mind).

The mind is such because of objects.

Each exists only as it is relative to the other.

In the Balance the two are indistinguishable

and each contains in itself all that is.

If we do not discriminate between coarse and fine

we will not be drawn into prejudice and opinion.

12

Living the Beauty Way is neither easy nor difficult.

Only when we limit ourselves with illusion and opinion

do we grow fearful and indecisive.

The faster we hurry, the slower we go.

The more we cling (attachment), the more we lose our path.

Even attachment to the idea of gaining Balance

will take us astray.

13

Let things be as they are intended
and they neither stay nor go; they merely flow.
Honor the nature of things (our own nature)
and we are in Balance with the Beauty Way;
we walk free and unmolested.

When we hold on to a thought, the truth is hidden.

Things become confusing and wrong.

And the burdensome practice of judging

brings irritation and weariness.

What is gained from distinctions and separations?

If we wish to dwell in the Beauty Way

let us not shun the senses and intuitions.

Indeed, to accept them fully

is to become the Beauty Way.

The wise man does not contrive a goal;
only the one enslaved by his ego
hobbles himself with such.

17

There is one Beauty Way, not many.

The others arise from the clinging needs of the ego.

To seek heart with the mind

is the greatest of all mistakes.

Peace and chaos, like and dislike,
and all other dualities, are illusions of the ego.
They are like flowers in the air
—foolish to try and grasp them.
Profit and loss, right and wrong,
let them go and be gone for good.

19

If the heart center never sleeps,
all dreams are the voice of heart.
If the mind does not discriminate,
the ten thousand things are one.

When we embrace this mystery
we are released from all entanglements.
To know all things in this way of oneness[23]
is to return to our natural state.
We cannot judge or compare
when all reason for separation has ceased.

Since stopping is movement without motion

and movement is rest without stopping,

both movement and rest disappear.

When such dualities cease to exist

Balance itself disappears.

No law or model

fits this primal clarity.[24]

When the heart thus becomes the Beauty Way
all ego-centered striving ceases.
Doubt and confusion vanish
and a life of clarity and passion emerges.
In a breath we are freed from our past,
with nothing clinging and nothing to remember.

23

All is vibrant, clear, and spontaneous
with no mental exertion.
Thought, anyway, would be useless
on what thought cannot fathom.

In this world of the Beauty Way

there is neither self nor other.

To come immediately into balance with the Way

when doubt arises just say "not two."

In this "not two," nothing is separate,

there is nothing that is not included.

The wise ones of all ages and places

have entered this source of truth.

This truth can be neither increased nor diminished,

for an instant of awareness is ten thousand years.

There is nowhere that truth is not,

as the infinite universe

is right before our eyes.

The minute is as large as the infinite
and the infinite is as small as the minute;
no eye can see before or beyond either.
So too it is with being and non-being.
We waste time with doubts and arguments
until we have grasped this awareness.

One thing is all things,

as all are the one flowing energy.

If we can embrace this truth

we no longer have to worry about the meaning of life.[25]

To the heart there is no duality,

and non-duality is the way to the heart.

29

This is where words fail,

as there is no more way to talk of it,

For it is not yesterday, tomorrow, or today.

A Word's Incredible Journey

THROUGH ETYMOLOGY, THE STUDY OF WORD ORIGINS, WE HAVE a way of finding the sources of thought and cultural characteristics, and then tracking their evolutions and migration patterns. Etymological research traces the word *Zen* back to the Sanskrit *dhyā-nam*, which means *an elevated state of consciousness leading to oneness.*[26] *Dhyānam* derives from the Indo-European root **dhyā-*: to see, look at.[27]

From the Indian subcontinent, derivatives of *dhyā* spread both East and West. In Greece, **dhyā-* became *sā-,* as in the Greek *sāma,* and then the Latin *signum.*[28] With trade, colonization, and conquest, these terms spread throughout the West to become the German *Zeichen,* the Russian *shak,* the Spanish *señal,* and the English *sign.*[29]

While these Western terms, having evolved in a secular environment, generally refer to an indication, symbol, or distinguishing mark, their Eastern counterparts retained the deeper significance of the Sanskrit dhyānam. In classical China, dhyānam became *chán* (禪), which changed to *thien* in Vietnam and the familiar *zen* in Japan.[30]

Layers of Meaning

The Art of Translating *Song of Trusting the Heart*

WHILE RESEARCHING *Song of Trusting the Heart*, I FOUND TWENTY
different versions of the title. Whether the original Chinese text
Xìnxīn Míng (信心銘) was translated by Eastern or Western scholars,
their translations varied from one another, sometimes significantly.
Here are examples:

Faith in Mind (Sheng-yen)
Trust Mind Inscription (Hae Kwang)
Words Inscribed on the Believing Mind (Heinrich Dumoulin)
The Mind of Absolute Trust (Stephen Mitchell)
Verses on the Faith Mind (Richard B. Clarke)
Poem on the Trust in the Heart (Thomas Cleary)

Why is this?
Translating is anything but an exact science. If it were, computers

would probably have taken over the translating profession by now. At best, computer translations read awkwardly, and some of them are downright humorous. Precise, word-for-word, human-rendered translations fare no better. I've seen some that were near incomprehensible.

Kahlil Gibran once said, "Translation is an art in itself; it is the re-creative process of transforming the magic of one language into the magic of another."[31] I doubt that artistic sense and magical touch are what most people imagine a translator needs. Yet these qualities are vital, as a translation must be artfully rendered in the current vernacular in order to touch the hearts and minds of its readers. Additionally, translators of material from other cultures or eras need the sensitivity of a poet, the perspective of a philosopher, and the cultural grounding of a sociologist, along with working knowledge of the subject matter. Imagine your confusion if you had no knowledge of Western culture or the English language and you read in your language a literal translation of the phrase *Rock 'n roll is here to stay*.

Without personally knowing the translators of the texts I was considering for the basis of my rendition of *Song of Trusting the Heart*, I had to determine their translating aptitude from their works. My study of classic Zen gave me the wherewithal to gauge their knowledge of culture and subject matter, and my experience as a storyteller helped me appraise their talent for magic.

Having chosen the five translations I found to be truest to the original, I selected the most precisely worded phrasing from each by comparing them line-for-line to each other and to the Chinese script. To clarify muddy passages, I broke characters down to their component parts. Characters often hold deeper meaning because they represent thoughts and ideas, whereas alphabet letters merely denote sounds. To illustrate an embedded meaning, I present my analysis of the title. The first line shows the title divided into its two character components. They can be further divided, as is shown in line two. This gives us the components' underlying meanings. One more split, as displayed in line three, bares the core concepts from which the title characters evolved.

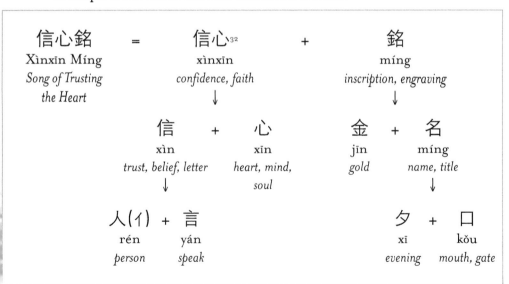

信心銘 = 信心[32] + 銘
Xìnxīn Míng   xìnxīn   míng
Song of Trusting   *confidence, faith*   *inscription, engraving*
the Heart   ↓   ↓

        信 + 心   金 + 名
        xìn   xīn   jīn   míng
trust, belief, letter *heart, mind,*   *gold*   *name, title*
                              soul   ↓
                               ↓

    人(亻) + 言   夕 + 口
    rén   yán   xī   kǒu
    person *speak*   *evening* *mouth, gate*

Other challenges to translation accuracy lie in the fact that classical-era characters have been simplified over time, and some of them have changed meanings (as also occurs in English, such as with *nice*, which meant "stupid" when it first entered the English language from French[33]). Add to this that Classical Chinese (like Latin) is a dead language, which gives no usage context for reference. The issue was present even in the time of the Táng Dynasty, as written and spoken Chinese were not entirely the same language. Each was evolving at a different pace and under a different set of influences.[34]

While undertaking the research for this book, I came to deeply respect translators for their multiple skills and talents. In particular, I am grateful for those who undertook the daunting task of translating *Xìnxīn Míng* and for the exemplary works they produced.

Suggested Reading

Depending on which Zen follower you ask, Zen can be an organized practice or it can be self-guided; and it either has a canon or it has no written scripture. Some believe it evolved fifteen hundred years ago as a Buddhist-influenced offshoot of Daoism (also commonly known as Taoism), and others say it was founded twenty-five hundred years ago by Siddhartha Gautama (the Buddha) himself. And then there is the question of label: is it Zen, Zen Buddhism, Buddhism, or Daoism? There are those who use two or more of these terms interchangeably and there are those who use them to denote distinct practices or religions. Sects (also called houses, schools, or forms) abound. On top of all that, Tibet, Mongolia, Thailand, China, Japan, Korea, and Vietnam each have their distinct traditions. Whew—where does someone with a curiosity for Zen begin?

Following are readings that I consider to be representative of the spectrum of Zen. They cover both philosophy and practice. To gain a good overview, you may want to select several books from this list.

The Spirit of Zen by Alan W. Watts, Grove Press, New York, 1958.

Zen for Beginners by Judith Blackstone and Zoran Jusipovic, Writers and Readers Publishing, New York, 1986.

Zen Keys by Thich Nhat Hanh, Image, New York, 1995.

Tao Te Ching by Lao Tzu, Vintage, New York, 1997.

The Elements of Taoism by Martin Palmer, Element, Boston, 1991.

Daoism Explained: From the Dream of the Butterfly to the Fishnet Allegory by Hans-Georg Moeller, Open Court, Chicago, 2004.

The Way to Freedom: Core Teachings of Tibetan Buddhism by the Dalai Lama and Donald S. Lopez, HarperCollins, New York, 1994.

Buddhism for Beginners by Thubten Chodron, Snow Lion, Ithaca, 2001.

Notes

[1] Richard B. Lee and Richard Daly, ed., *The Cambridge Encyclopedia of Hunters and Gatherers* (New York: Cambridge University Press, 1999), 1.

[2] Essence of Buddhism, Thich Thien-An, *Zen Philosophy, Zen Practice* (Berkeley: Dharma Publishing, 1975), 1.

[3] D.T. Suzuki, *An Introduction to Zen Buddhism* (New York: Grove Press, 1994), 33, 36.

[4] Suzuki, *An Introduction to Zen Buddhism*, 34; Alan W. Watts, *The Way of Zen*, (New York: Pantheon, 1999), 3.

[5] Suzuki, *An Introduction to Zen Buddhism*, 35.

[6] Many variations exist; R. H. Blyth's *Zen and Zen Classics: Volume One* (Tokyo: Hokuseido Press, 1960), 47.

[7] Hallmarks of religion, as opposed to spirituality, which *Webster's New International Dictionary*, 2nd ed. defines as incorporeal; that is, not having a material body or form…not being an object of sense; Formal studies, Watts, *The Spirit of Zen*, 18; Observances,

Random House Webster's Unabridged Dictionary, 2nd ed., s.v. "zen"; Teachers, Goddard, *A Buddhist Bible* (Boston: Beacon Press, 1994), 8.

[8] Alan W. Watts, *The Spirit of Zen,* (New York: Grove Press Inc., 1958), 22.

[9] Also translated as *Inscription on Trust in the Mind* (Burton Watson); *Inscribed on the Believing Mind* (Daisetsu Teitart Suzuki); *Verses on the Faith Mind* (Richard B. Clarke). These translations were found at the Internet Sacred Text Archive, www.sacredtexts.com/bud/zen/fm/fm.htm.

[10] R.H. Blyth, *Zen and Zen Classics Vol. 1* (Tokyo: Hokuseido Press, 1960).

[11] Jack Kornfield, *Teachings of the Buddha* (Boston: Shambhala, 1996).

[12] Aldous Huxley, *The Perennial Philosophy* (New York: Perennial Books, 1990).

[13] Christopher Cullen, *Astronomy and Mathematics in Ancient China: The Zhou bi suan jing* (Cambridge: Cambridge University Press, 2007).

[14] Edwin F. Bryant, *The Yoga Sūtras of Patañjali* (New York: North Point Press, 2009), xxvii.

[15] Thelma Hall, r.c., *Too Deep for Words: Rediscovering Lectio Divina* (Mahwah: Paulist Press, 1988), 28.

[16] Shaykh Khwaja Shamsuddin Azeemi, *Muraqaba: The Art and Science of Sufi Meditation* (Houston: Plato Publishing, Inc., 2005), 54.

[17] Nan Fink Gefen, *Discovering Jewish Meditation: Instruction & Guidance for Learning an Ancient Spiritual Practice* (Woodstock: Jewish Lights Publishing, 1999), 31.

[18] Yasunari Kawabata, *Japan the Beautiful and Myself* (New York: Kodansha America, 1981), 54.

[19] Also translated as Perfect Way, Great Way, Ultimate Way.

[20] Also translated as *mind*.

[21] Also translated as *serenity, equanimity, peace*.

[22] Also translated as *essence, source*.

[23] Also translated as *with equal mind*.

[24] Also translated as *ultimate consummation, in their finality*.

[25] Also translated as *perfect knowledge*.

[26] Watts, *The Spirit of Zen*, 24.

[27] *The American Heritage Dictionary of the English Language*, 4th ed., s.v. "zen."

[28] *The Classic Latin Dictionary* (Chicago: Follett, 1941), s.v. "sign."

[29] *Oxford-Duden German Dictionary* (New York: Oxford University Press, 1990), s.v. "zeichen"; *Romanov's Russian-English Dictionary* (New York: Pocket Books, 1964), s.v. "sign"; *Oxford Spanish Dictionary*, 3rd ed. (Oxford: Oxford University Press, 2003), s.v. "señal"; *Random House Dictionary*, s.v. "zen."

[30] Thich Thien-An, *Zen Philosophy, Zen Practice* (Berkeley: Dharma Publishing, 1975), 2; *The Shorter Oxford English Dictionary*, 5th ed., s.v. "zen."

[31] Kahlil Gibran, *Prose Poems by Kahlil Gibran* (New York: Alfred A. Knopf, Inc.,1934), v.

[32] *Chinese Dictionary* (Hong Kong: Oxford University Press (China), 2003), s.vv. "xìnxīn (信心)," "xìn (信)," "xīn (心)," "rén (人)," "yán (言)," "míng (銘)," "jīn (金)," "míng (名)," "xī (夕)," "kǒu (口)."

[33] Eric Partridge, *Origins: A Short Etymological History of the English Language* (New York: Greenwich House, 1983), 594; John Ayto, *Dictionary of Word Origins* (New York: Arcade Publishing, 1990), 364.

[34] Jerry Norman, *Chinese* (Cambridge: Cambridge University Press, 1988), 1-2.

FOLLOWING HIS TIME AS A ROMAN Catholic seminarian, Tamarack Song was introduced to Zen by the works of Alan Watts. Shortly thereafter, Tamarack gave up his considerable wealth and took life-time vows of poverty and service. He then devoted forty years to study and reflection on the world's religions, languages, and indigenous cultures. Continually impressed by how the tenets of Zen kept appearing in unrelated traditions, he came to realize Zen's universality.

"I discovered," says Tamarack, "that the essence of Zen is listening." Through writing and teaching, he dedicates his life to helping people awaken their deep listening skills. At the Teaching Drum Outdoor School, which he founded, seekers from around the world come to learn how to return to essential being (the ageless Zen approach) in their modern-day lives. Tamarack provides an idyllic, distraction-free, and intensely challenging un-learning environment by taking seekers into the wilderness for a year of aboriginal living—the only such experience offered in America or Europe.

Tamarack is also the author of *Journey to the Ancestral Self* and *Whispers of the Ancients*. Information on his courses and writings can be found at www.teachingdrum.org.

The Artist

Jan Zaremba regrets not being able to find a single decent picture of himself. "But this one," he says, "comes pretty close to the truth." Born in Germany, he emigrated to the US to study engineering. He then studied painting with the German Expressionist Schwaderer. Afterwards, he lived for three years in a monastery to study Advaita Vedanta. All this, he maintains, was preparation for meeting Hisashi Ohta, Zen Master and Living National Treasure of Japan. After two years of intense practice, Ohta pronounced his student a Master of Sumi-e, and after another year Ohta gave his Japanese students to Zaremba and made him Sensei. The widow of his master studied sumi-e with Zaremba for the next fifteen years. Now the seventy-year-old artist lives on the East Coast. His works have been exhibited in Germany, Finland, Mexico, Korea, and Japan. He has never owned a TV.

More paintings at www.janzaremba.com.

Sentient Publications, LLC publishes books on cultural creativity, experimental education, transformative spirituality, holistic health, new science, ecology, and other topics, approached from an integral viewpoint. Our authors are intensely interested in exploring the nature of life from fresh perspectives, addressing life's great questions, and fostering the full expression of the human potential. Sentient Publications' books arise from the spirit of inquiry and the richness of the inherent dialogue between writer and reader.

Our Culture Tools series is designed to give social catalyzers and cultural entrepreneurs the essential information, technology, and inspiration to forge a sustainable, creative, and compassionate world.

We are very interested in hearing from our readers. To direct suggestions or comments to us, or to be added to our mailing list, please contact:

SENTIENT PUBLICATIONS, LLC
1113 Spruce Street
Boulder, CO 80302
303-443-2188
contact@sentientpublications.com
www.sentientpublications.com